SOUTHERN IRELAND TRAVEL GUIDE

Embark on a journey through the emerald landscapes of Southern Ireland, where ancient castles whisper tales of history, vibrant cities pulse with lively traditions, and the warmth of local hospitality invites you to savor the enchanting beauty of the Emerald Isle.

Copyright © Eric Lot 2024

All rights reserved. No part of this book may be reproduced or transmitted in any form or by any means, electronic or mechanical, including photocopying, recording, or by any information storage and retrieval system, without written permission from the author, except for the inclusion of brief quotations in a review.

Disclaimer

The information provided in this book is designed to provide helpful information on the subjects discussed. The guidebook is only meant to provide the reader with the basics travel guidelines of a certain location, without any warranties regarding the accuracy of the information and advice provided. Each traveler should do their own research before departing.

Please be sure to research the places you plan to visit before you go. You can find images and maps online.

Contents

CHAPTER ONE **6**
  INTRODUCTION TO SOUTHERN IRELAND 6
    Overview of Southern Ireland 6
    Geography and Climate 7
    Cultural and Historical Significance 9

CHAPTER TWO **11**
  PLANNING YOUR BUDGET TRIP 11
    Budget Travel Tips 11
    Cost-Saving Strategies 13
    Transportation Options 16

CHAPTER THREE **21**
  ACCOMMODATION ON A BUDGET 21
    Affordable Accommodation Options 21
    Hostels, Guesthouses, and B&Bs 24
    Camping and Alternative Lodging 28

CHAPTER FOUR **32**
  EXPLORING SOUTHERN IRELAND'S CULINARY SCENE 32
    Introduction to Irish Cuisine 32
    Budget-Friendly Dining Options 35
    Street Food and Markets 39

CHAPTER FIVE **43**
  MUST-TRY LOCAL DISHES 43

Traditional Irish Dishes 43
Regional Specialties 46
Vegetarian and Vegan Options 49

CHAPTER SIX **53**
BUDGET-FRIENDLY ACTIVITIES AND ATTRACTIONS 53
Free and Low-Cost Attractions 53
Outdoor Activities on a Budget 56
Cultural Experiences without Breaking the Bank 60

CHAPTER SEVEN **64**
BUDGET-FRIENDLY TRAVEL ITINERARIES 64
One-Week Budget Itinerary for Southern Ireland 64
Two-Week Budget Itinerary for Southern Ireland 68
Customizing Your Itinerary 73

CHAPTER EIGHT **79**
MONEY-SAVING TRAVEL HACKS 79
Discounts and Deals 79
Budget-Friendly Shopping Tips 83
Saving on Souvenirs 88

CHAPTER NINE **93**
SAFETY TIPS FOR BUDGET TRAVELERS 93
Staying Safe in Southern Ireland 93
Emergency Contacts and Resources 97

CHAPTER TEN **103**

USEFUL RESOURCES 103

    Budget Travel Websites 103

    Recommended Reading 108

CHAPTER ELEVEN 113

    CONCLUSION 113

    Encouragement for Budget Travelers 113

    Resources for Further Exploration 117

CHAPTER ONE

INTRODUCTION TO SOUTHERN IRELAND

Overview of Southern Ireland

Welcome to the enchanting realm of Southern Ireland, where lush green landscapes meet rugged coastlines and charming towns steeped in history. Picture rolling hills dotted with sheep, ancient castles standing as silent witnesses to bygone eras, and vibrant cities buzzing with culture and warmth.

Southern Ireland, also known as the "Emerald Isle," is renowned for its stunning natural beauty, captivating folklore, and rich cultural heritage. From the windswept cliffs of Moher to the serene lakes of Killarney National Park, every corner of this region beckons with its own unique allure.

Immerse yourself in the warmth of Irish hospitality as you journey through quaint villages adorned with colorful facades and cobblestone streets. Discover the tales of ancient kings and legendary saints, woven into the fabric of Southern Ireland's past and present.

Whether you're exploring the bustling streets of Dublin, savoring the tranquility of the countryside, or tracing the footsteps of literary giants like James Joyce and W.B. Yeats, Southern Ireland promises a tapestry of experiences that will leave you enchanted and longing for more. So pack your sense of adventure and get ready to embark on a journey like no other in the heart of Southern Ireland.

Geography and Climate

Dive into the diverse tapestry of Southern Ireland's geography and climate, where Mother Nature herself seems to showcase her artistic prowess. The landscape here is a patchwork quilt of emerald green fields, craggy coastlines, and misty mountains, creating a breathtaking panorama that evolves with every turn of the road.

Southern Ireland's geography is a fascinating blend of contrasts. From the rugged peaks of the Macgillycuddy's Reeks in County Kerry to the serene lakes nestled in the valleys, each region boasts its own unique charm. The meandering rivers and rolling hills contribute to an ever-changing scenery that feels like stepping into a living postcard.

Now, let's talk about the climate – a delightful dance between sunshine and rain. Southern Ireland experiences a temperate maritime climate, ensuring that you might experience all four seasons in a single day. The gentle mist that kisses your face one moment can give way to bright sunshine, making each weather change a surprise waiting to unfold.

As you traverse this picturesque terrain, be prepared for the unexpected and embrace the beauty of Southern Ireland's ever-shifting weather patterns. From the cozy warmth of traditional pubs on rainy days to basking in the sunlight along the Cliffs of Moher, the geography and climate of

Southern Ireland create a dynamic backdrop for your unforgettable adventure.

Cultural and Historical Significance

Step into the heart of Southern Ireland's cultural tapestry, where every stone, song, and story speaks of a rich and captivating history. The cultural and historical significance of this region is not just a chapter in a book; it's a living, breathing narrative that unfolds as you explore its ancient landmarks and engage with its vibrant traditions.

Southern Ireland wears its history with pride, from the ancient monastic sites like Glendalough, where whispers of monks from centuries past linger in the air, to the imposing Rock of Cashel, an iconic silhouette against the sky that tells tales of kings and conquests.

The warmth of the Irish people is a testament to a culture shaped by centuries of shared stories, music, and dance. Whether you find yourself in a lively pub session in Galway, tapping your feet to traditional tunes, or attending a local festival celebrating age-old customs, you'll quickly realize that Southern Ireland's cultural vibrancy is a celebration of its people.

The historical significance unfolds in the narrow lanes of medieval towns, where castle walls echo with the footsteps of knights and maidens. The ancient manuscripts and illuminated texts housed in libraries reveal a literary heritage that has stood the test of time.

In every pub, in every conversation, and in every castle's stone, Southern Ireland's cultural and historical significance invites you to become part of a narrative that continues to evolve. So, prepare to be immersed in the living history of a land where every day feels like a page turned in a captivating story.

CHAPTER TWO

PLANNING YOUR BUDGET TRIP

Budget Travel Tips

Embark on your Southern Ireland adventure with a savvy mindset and a pocket-friendly approach. Navigating the emerald landscapes on a budget is not only possible but also adds an extra layer of excitement to your journey. Here are some tried-and-true budget travel tips to ensure you make the most of every penny:

1. **Off-Peak Magic:** Discover the enchantment of Southern Ireland during off-peak seasons. Not only will you avoid crowds, but accommodations and attractions often offer discounted rates, allowing you to experience the beauty of the region without breaking the bank.

2. **Budget-Friendly Accommodations:** Embrace the charm of guesthouses, B&Bs, and hostels scattered across Southern Ireland. These accommodations not only

provide an authentic Irish experience but are often more affordable than traditional hotels. Bonus: they come with local insights and warm hospitality.

3. Public Transport Prowess: Navigate the Irish landscapes with cost-effective public transportation. Buses and trains not only connect major cities but also offer scenic routes through the countryside. Consider purchasing multi-day passes for added savings.

4. Picnic Pleasures: Immerse yourself in the local culture by grabbing fresh produce from farmers' markets or local shops and indulging in a delightful picnic. Not only is it a budget-friendly dining option, but it also allows you to savor the flavors of Southern Ireland in scenic settings.

5. Free Walking Tours: Lace up your walking shoes and explore cities like Dublin, Cork, and Galway with free walking tours. Knowledgeable guides will lead you through historical landmarks, sharing tales of the past without denting your budget.

6. Cultural Exchange: Dive into the heart of Southern Ireland's culture by attending local events and festivals. Many of these experiences are free or low-cost, offering a glimpse into the traditions, music, and dance that make the region truly special.

7. Pack a Picnic: Save on meals by packing a picnic for your day's adventures. Find a scenic spot, unfurl your blanket, and enjoy the breathtaking views along with your budget-friendly feast.

These budget travel tips are your key to unlocking the treasures of Southern Ireland without burning a hole in your wallet. So, pack your enthusiasm, a sense of adventure, and get ready for a budget-friendly journey through the captivating landscapes of the Emerald Isle.

Cost-Saving Strategies

Southern Ireland's allure doesn't have to come with a hefty price tag. Embrace a frugal mindset and unleash the adventurer in you with these clever cost-saving strategies. From accommodations to daily expenses, discover ways to maximize your experience without draining your funds:

1. Accommodation Alternatives: Beyond traditional lodgings, explore the world of alternative accommodations. From charming Airbnb stays to rural farmhouses, Southern Ireland offers unique and budget-friendly options that add a touch of authenticity to your journey.

2. Grocery Store Adventures: Dive into local grocery stores for a budget-friendly feast. Stock up on essentials, fresh produce, and Irish delicacies to create your own meals. It's not just economical; it's a chance to savor the flavors of Southern Ireland at your own pace.

3. Attractions Bundle: Invest in attraction bundles or passes that offer discounted entry fees to multiple sites. Whether you're exploring historic castles or natural wonders, these bundles can significantly reduce individual costs and make your adventure more affordable.

4. DIY Day Tours: Craft your own day tours by utilizing public transportation and creating personalized itineraries. This not only gives you the flexibility to explore at your own pace but also allows you to tailor your experiences to match your budget.

5. Tap into Local Wisdom: Connect with locals for insider tips on hidden gems and budget-friendly activities. From lesser-known hiking trails to charming cafes, the people of Southern Ireland are eager to share their favorite spots, often away from the tourist traps.

6. Student and Youth Discounts: If you're a student or a young traveler, take advantage of the numerous discounts available. From transportation to attractions, flashing your student or youth ID can unlock a world of savings.

7. BYOB Adventures: Opt for BYOB (Bring Your Own Bottle) when dining out. Many restaurants allow patrons to bring their own wine or beer, saving you money on pricey drinks while still enjoying the local culinary scene.

8. Budget-Friendly Events: Keep an eye out for budget-friendly events and festivals happening during your visit. These cultural celebrations often offer free or low-cost entertainment, allowing you to immerse yourself in the vibrant spirit of Southern Ireland without breaking the bank.

These cost-saving strategies are your passport to a budget-friendly exploration of Southern Ireland. So, pack your enthusiasm, a sprinkle of resourcefulness, and get ready to savor the magic of the Emerald Isle without emptying your wallet.

Transportation Options

Embark on a seamless journey through Southern Ireland by exploring the diverse transportation options that connect this enchanting region. Whether you prefer the scenic route or a swift city hop, these transportation choices ensure you navigate the Emerald Isle with ease, all while keeping your budget intact.

1. Public Transport Prowess: Dive into the heart of Irish communities with the extensive public transportation network. Buses operated by Bus Éireann (www.buseireann.ie) and trains managed by Irish Rail (www.irishrail.ie) crisscross the landscapes, providing an affordable and picturesque means of exploring Southern Ireland. Choose from single tickets, day passes, or multi-day options for added flexibility.

2. Budget-Friendly Car Rentals: For those seeking the freedom of the open road, consider budget-friendly car rentals from companies like Europcar (www.europcar.ie) or Hertz (www.hertz.ie). Roam at your own pace, unveiling hidden gems tucked away in the countryside. Compare prices, book in advance, and be prepared for a road trip filled with breathtaking landscapes.

3. Hitchhiking Adventures: Channel your inner adventurer and embrace the time-honored tradition of hitchhiking. While not as common as in the past, Southern Ireland maintains a friendly atmosphere, making hitchhiking a unique and cost-effective way to connect with locals and fellow travelers. Exercise caution and use platforms like Hitchwiki (www.hitchwiki.org) for safety tips and hitchhiking locations.

4. Cycling Excursions: Take a spin through the emerald landscapes on two wheels. Southern Ireland's scenic routes and designated cycling paths make cycling an eco-friendly and budget-conscious option. Rent a bike locally from shops like Cycle Ireland (www.cycleireland.ie) or bring your own for a leisurely exploration.

5. Shared Rides and Carpooling: Join the eco-conscious movement of shared rides and carpooling. Platforms like BlaBlaCar (www.blablacar.ie) allow you to connect with drivers heading in your direction, reducing travel costs and fostering new connections along the way.

6. Domestic Flights Insights: When time is of the essence, explore domestic flights for longer journeys. While Southern Ireland's size makes flying less common, it can be a convenient option for hopping between major cities. Airlines like Aer Lingus (www.aerlingus.com) and Ryanair (www.ryanair.com) offer domestic flights, providing a faster travel alternative.

7. Wander by Foot: Lace up your walking shoes and embrace the charm of Southern Ireland on foot. Many towns and cities are pedestrian-friendly, encouraging leisurely strolls to discover hidden corners, local shops, and vibrant street scenes. Check out walking tour options offered by local guides or tourist information centers for a guided exploration.

8. Ferry Tales: Connect with the coastal beauty of Southern Ireland by incorporating ferry rides into your itinerary. Explore islands, coastal villages, and peninsulas, creating a memorable journey that combines scenic waterways with budget-friendly travel. Companies like Irish Ferries (www.irishferries.com) and Stena Line (www.stenaline.ie) offer ferry services connecting various ports in Southern Ireland.

Choose the transportation mode that aligns with your travel style, and let the journey through Southern Ireland unfold with each delightful mile. These diverse options ensure that every traveler can navigate the emerald landscapes with both convenience and affordability in mind.

CHAPTER THREE

ACCOMMODATION ON A BUDGET

Affordable Accommodation Options

Immerse yourself in the cozy embrace of Southern Ireland without breaking the bank by exploring a range of affordable accommodation options. From charming guesthouses to budget-friendly hostels, these choices not only offer a comfortable stay but also provide an authentic Irish experience.

1. Guesthouses with Character: Delve into the heart of Southern Irish hospitality by opting for guesthouses that exude charm and character. Places like Gleeson's Townhouse in Roscommon (www.gleesonstownhouse.com) or Dunraven Arms Hotel in Adare (www.dunravenhotel.com) offer affordable yet delightful stays, where warm welcomes and personalized service make you feel right at home.

2. Quaint Bed and Breakfasts (B&Bs): Experience the warmth of Irish hospitality with a stay at one of the many quaint Bed and Breakfasts scattered across Southern Ireland. Places like Ardmore House in Clifden (www.ardmorehouse.com) or Drumcreehy Country House in Ballyvaughan (www.drumcreehyhouse.com) provide not only a budget-friendly stay but also a chance to connect with local hosts who are eager to share insider tips.

3. Hostel Havens: For the budget-conscious traveler, hostels are a fantastic option. Stay in the heart of vibrant cities or amidst the tranquility of the countryside. Hostelworld (www.hostelworld.com) can help you find affordable gems like Kinlay House in Galway or Barnacles Hostel in Dublin, where communal spaces foster connections with fellow travelers.

4. Countryside Camping: Embrace nature and keep costs low by camping in the beautiful Southern Irish countryside. Camping sites like Actons Beachside Camping in Connemara (www.actonsbeachsidecamping.com) or Eagle Point Camping in Bantry (www.eaglepointcamping.com) offer a serene retreat under the stars, letting you wake up to the beauty of the Emerald Isle.

5. Unique Airbnb Finds: Explore the uniqueness of Southern Ireland with budget-friendly Airbnb options. Whether it's a traditional Irish cottage in the hills or a city-center apartment, Airbnb (www.airbnb.com) provides a variety of affordable and distinctive accommodation choices that suit different preferences.

6. Budget-Friendly Inns: Uncover the charm of budget-friendly inns that offer a comfortable stay without the hefty price tag. Places like The Valley Hotel in Fivemiletown (www.thevalleyhotel.com) or The Castle Hotel in Macroom (www.castlehotel.ie) provide a blend of affordability and local charm.

7. Farmhouse Retreats: Experience the tranquility of Southern Ireland's rural life with a stay on a farmhouse. Farms like

Ballymaloe House in Shanagarry (www.ballymaloe.ie) or Rathbaun Farm in Aran Islands (www.rathbaunfarm.com) offer a unique and budget-friendly accommodation experience, complete with a glimpse into Irish farm life.

Southern Ireland's affordable accommodation options cater to every traveler's taste and budget, ensuring that your stay is not just comfortable but adds an extra layer of authenticity to your Irish adventure.

Hostels, Guesthouses, and B&Bs

Dive into the heart of Southern Ireland's charm by exploring a trifecta of affordable and welcoming accommodations – hostels, guesthouses, and bed-and-breakfasts (B&Bs). Each option not only offers budget-friendly stays but also provides a unique opportunity to connect with the local culture and hospitality.

1. Hostels for Social Sojourns: For the budget-savvy traveler seeking camaraderie, hostels in Southern Ireland are a fantastic choice. Hostelworld (www.hostelworld.com) unveils a spectrum of options, from lively urban hubs to peaceful countryside retreats. Consider Kinlay House in Galway or Abbey Court in Dublin for an affordable stay with communal spaces that foster connections with fellow adventurers.

2. Quaint Guesthouses: Guesthouses in Southern Ireland are synonymous with warmth and character. Opt for these cozy havens to enjoy a personalized experience, often hosted by locals passionate about sharing their region. Gleeson's Townhouse in Roscommon (www.gleesonstownhouse.com) or Lough Inagh Lodge in Connemara (www.loughinaghlodgehotel.ie) are perfect examples where affordability meets charm.

3. Bed-and-Breakfast Bliss: Uncover the true essence of Irish hospitality by staying in one of the many Bed-and-Breakfasts scattered across Southern Ireland. Ardmore House in Clifden (www.ardmorehouse.com) or Cahergal Farmhouse in Newmarket-on-Fergus (www.cahergal.com) provide a cozy retreat, often accompanied by hearty Irish breakfasts and local insights from welcoming hosts.

4. Cultural Exchange at B&Bs: Bed-and-Breakfasts not only offer a comfortable bed for the night but also create an intimate space for cultural exchange. Choose places like Drumcreehy Country House in Ballyvaughan (www.drumcreehyhouse.com) or Currarevagh House in Oughterard (www.currarevagh.com) for an immersive experience, where hosts share stories, tips, and a slice of their Southern Irish life.

5. Coastal Retreats: Southern Ireland's coastline is dotted with charming hostels, guesthouses, and B&Bs that provide stunning sea views and proximity to coastal wonders. Check out the YHA hostels like Knockree Hostel in Enniskerry (www.hostelworld.com/hostel-details/knockree-hostel/enniskerry/1472) or Cliff House in Ardmore (www.cliffhousehotel.ie) for an affordable seaside stay.

6. Urban Hostels for City Explorations: Immerse yourself in the vibrant atmosphere of Southern Ireland's cities by choosing urban hostels. Barnacles Hostel in Dublin or Sleepzone Hostel in Galway offer budget-friendly accommodations in the heart of cultural hubs, allowing you to explore the city's attractions without straining your wallet.

7. Personalized Attention at Guesthouses: Guesthouses in Southern Ireland often pride themselves on personalized attention and local expertise. Discover the allure of places like Dunraven Arms Hotel in Adare (www.dunravenhotel.com) or Roundwood House in Mountrath (www.roundwoodhouse.com), where attentive hosts elevate your stay with insider tips and genuine Irish hospitality.

Southern Ireland's hostels, guesthouses, and B&Bs form a mosaic of affordable accommodation options, each contributing to a memorable and authentic experience. Whether you seek social interactions, cozy retreats, or personalized attention, these choices promise a comfortable stay with a touch of Irish warmth.

Camping and Alternative Lodging

For those adventurers seeking a closer connection to nature, Southern Ireland opens its arms to camping enthusiasts and advocates of alternative lodging. Embrace the great outdoors or indulge in unique accommodations that go beyond the traditional, promising an unforgettable and budget-friendly experience.

1. Camping Bliss: Pitch your tent under the star-studded Southern Irish sky and wake up to the sounds of nature. Camping sites like Actons Beachside Camping in Connemara (www.actonsbeachsidecamping.com) or Eagle Point Camping in Bantry (www.eaglepointcamping.com) offer picturesque settings, making your camping experience an integral part of your Southern Ireland adventure.

2. Glamping Getaways: For a touch of luxury amidst nature, consider glamping (glamorous camping). Experience the tranquility of the countryside in comfort with options like Purecamping in Loop Head (www.purecamping.ie) or Teapot Lane Glamping in Leitrim (www.teapotlaneglamping.com), where cozy yurts, safari tents, or treehouses provide a unique and budget-friendly retreat.

3. Quirky Airbnb Retreats: Southern Ireland's alternative lodging scene is adorned with unique and quirky Airbnb options. Stay in a traditional Irish cottage, a converted barn, or a treehouse nestled in the woods. Airbnb (www.airbnb.com) showcases accommodations like the Blackbird Treehouse in Galway or the Hobbit Hut in Cork, promising a stay as memorable as the surrounding landscapes.

4. Coastal Campsites: The Southern Irish coastline beckons campers with stunning views and refreshing sea breezes. Choose coastal campsites such as Wave Crest Caravan and Camping Park in Caherdaniel (www.wavecrestcamping.com) or Sandycove Camping in Kinsale (www.sandycovecamping.com) for a seaside retreat that combines camping charm with proximity to the ocean.

5. Lighthouse Lodgings: For a truly unique experience, consider staying in alternative lodgings such as lighthouses. Accommodations like Wicklow Head Lighthouse (www.irishlandmark.com/property/wicklow-head-lighthouse) provide an extraordinary backdrop for your Southern Ireland adventure, offering both a historical and budget-friendly stay.

6. Eco-Friendly Stays: Connect with nature responsibly by opting for eco-friendly accommodations. Places like The Hollies in Enniskeane (www.thehollies.ie) focus on sustainability and provide budget-friendly lodging options, ensuring your stay aligns with your commitment to minimizing your environmental footprint.

7. Treehouse Retreats: Fulfill childhood dreams by staying in a treehouse amidst the Southern Irish woodlands. Treehouse accommodations, such as those found at Finn Lough in Fermanagh (www.finnlough.com), offer a whimsical and affordable escape, where the rustling leaves and birdsong become your companions.

Southern Ireland's camping and alternative lodging options cater to the free spirits and nature lovers, offering an array of choices that blend affordability with unique experiences. Whether you opt for a tent under the stars, a glamping haven, or a treehouse retreat, these alternatives promise a memorable stay in harmony with the stunning landscapes of the Emerald Isle.

CHAPTER FOUR

EXPLORING SOUTHERN IRELAND'S CULINARY SCENE

Introduction to Irish Cuisine

Prepare your taste buds for a culinary journey through the heart and soul of Southern Ireland as we delve into the rich tapestry of Irish cuisine. Rooted in tradition, the flavors of Ireland are a delightful blend of hearty, comforting, and locally sourced ingredients, reflecting the island's agricultural abundance and coastal treasures.

1. Homey Comforts: Irish cuisine is synonymous with comfort food that warms the soul. From steaming bowls of hearty stews to comforting potato dishes, the meals are designed to provide sustenance and warmth, often with recipes passed down through generations.

2. Potatoes in Every Form: No exploration of Irish cuisine is complete without acknowledging the central role of potatoes. Boiled, mashed, fried, or baked – the versatile potato takes various forms on Irish tables, forming the foundation for many iconic dishes like colcannon and champ.

3. Seafood Extravaganza: With a coastline kissed by the Atlantic Ocean, Irish cuisine celebrates the bounty of the sea. Indulge in fresh seafood delights such as succulent oysters, buttery smoked salmon, and hearty fish and chips, showcasing the maritime influence on the island's culinary identity.

4. Traditional Irish Breakfast: Start your day the Irish way with a traditional Irish breakfast. This hearty meal includes bacon, sausages, black and white pudding, eggs, and grilled tomatoes – a robust feast that provides the energy needed for a day of exploration.

5. Savory Pies and Pastries: Irish cuisine boasts a variety of savory pies and pastries, each filled with delicious combinations of meats, vegetables, and rich gravies. From steak and Guinness pies to flaky pastries stuffed with locally sourced ingredients, these dishes showcase the comfort and simplicity of Irish cooking.

6. Wholesome Breads: Ireland's bread-making traditions are woven into the fabric of its culinary heritage. Savor the aroma of freshly baked soda bread, brown bread, and traditional wheaten bread, often served with a generous dollop of creamy Irish butter.

7. Pubs and Culinary Atmosphere: Irish pubs are more than just places to enjoy a pint; they are hubs of culinary experiences. Many pubs offer hearty pub grub, featuring classics like beef and Guinness stew, bangers and mash, and delectable Irish lamb dishes. The convivial atmosphere enhances the dining experience, creating a perfect fusion of food and community.

8. Dairy Delights: Ireland's lush green pastures are home to happy cows, and the result is an abundance of high-quality dairy products. From rich and creamy Irish butter to artisanal cheeses, Irish dairy delights add a flavorful touch to many traditional dishes.

As you embark on your culinary exploration of Southern Ireland, be prepared to be captivated by the simplicity, authenticity, and heartiness that define Irish cuisine. Whether enjoying a meal in a cozy pub or savoring the delights of a farmhouse kitchen, the flavors of Southern Ireland will undoubtedly leave an indelible mark on your taste buds.

Budget-Friendly Dining Options

Embark on a gastronomic adventure through Southern Ireland without denting your wallet by exploring the diverse array of budget-friendly dining options. From charming local eateries to street food delights, the Emerald Isle offers a myriad of culinary experiences that are not only delicious but also gentle on your budget.

1. Local Cafés and Bakeries: Immerse yourself in the charm of Southern Ireland's local cafés and bakeries, where you can savor freshly brewed coffee and indulge in affordable treats. These cozy establishments often showcase homemade pastries, sandwiches, and snacks, providing a delightful and budget-friendly respite during your explorations. Example: Café Beva in Galway (www.cafebeva.com).

2. Pub Grub Magic: Discover the heart and soul of Irish cuisine at the local pubs, where hearty pub grub awaits. Dive into classics like beef and Guinness stew, traditional Irish stew, or a satisfying plate of bangers and mash. Pubs often offer affordable lunch specials, making them an excellent choice for a satisfying and economical meal. Example: The Brazen Head in Dublin (www.brazenhead.com).

3. Street Food Delights: Wander through the bustling streets of cities like Dublin, Galway, or Cork, and let your senses be enticed by the aroma of street food. From savory crepes and gourmet sandwiches to ethnic delights, Southern Ireland's street food scene provides a budget-friendly feast for those on the go. Example: Box Burger in Bray (www.boxburger.ie).

4. Farmers' Market Finds: Immerse yourself in the vibrant atmosphere of farmers' markets, where you can sample and purchase local produce, artisanal products, and budget-friendly bites. Many markets offer a variety of street food stalls, allowing you to create a personalized and economical tasting journey. Example: The English Market in Cork (www.englishmarket.ie).

5. Dine Early for Deals: Take advantage of early bird specials offered by many restaurants. Dining early not only allows you to enjoy a quieter atmosphere but often comes with discounted menus, providing an excellent opportunity to savor local cuisine at a fraction of the regular cost. Example: The Church Café Bar in Dublin (www.thechurch.ie).

6. Hidden Gems in Side Streets: Venture away from the main thoroughfares and explore the side streets to uncover hidden culinary gems. These local eateries often offer affordable and authentic dishes, providing a more intimate and budget-friendly dining experience. Example: The

Winding Stair in Dublin (www.winding-stair.com).

7. Student-Friendly Fare: If you're a student, make the most of student-friendly deals offered by restaurants and cafés. Many establishments near universities or popular student areas provide discounts, allowing you to enjoy delicious meals without straining your budget. Example: The Roost Café Bar in Maynooth (www.theroost.ie).

8. Takeaway Triumphs: Embrace the Irish tradition of takeaways, where you can enjoy a budget-friendly meal in the comfort of your accommodation or a scenic outdoor spot. Options range from fish and chips to delicious Indian or Chinese takeout, providing a convenient and economical dining alternative. Example: Beshoff Bros in Dublin (www.beshoffbros.com).

Southern Ireland's culinary landscape is not just about exquisite dining; it's a celebration of flavors accessible to every budget. Whether you opt for a hearty pub meal, explore street food markets, or indulge in local cafés, the budget-friendly dining options in Southern Ireland promise to satisfy your palate without breaking the bank.

Street Food and Markets

Embark on a flavorful journey through the lively streets and bustling markets of Southern Ireland, where street food vendors and market stalls beckon with an array of delectable delights. Savor the eclectic mix of local and international flavors as you explore these vibrant corners of culinary exploration.

1. Food Truck Delights: Navigate the charming streets of cities like Dublin, Cork, or Galway, where food trucks and stalls offer a diverse selection of street food. From gourmet burgers and artisanal pizzas to international cuisines, these mobile kitchens provide a budget-friendly feast for those seeking a quick and delicious culinary adventure.

2. Temple Bar Food Market, Dublin: Dive into the heart of Dublin's Temple Bar Food Market, a bustling weekend destination for food enthusiasts. Sample artisanal cheeses, freshly baked pastries, and international street food, all while soaking in the lively atmosphere. (Location: Meeting House Square, Temple Bar, Dublin)

3. English Market, Cork: Explore the historic English Market in Cork, where food stalls showcase the best of local produce and international flavors. From fresh seafood and gourmet cheeses to artisan chocolates, the market is a treasure trove for food lovers. (Location: Princes Street, Cork City)

4. Galway Market, Galway: Immerse yourself in the vibrant Galway Market, a lively hub of activity offering an array of fresh produce, handmade crafts, and, of course, mouthwatering street food. Indulge in global cuisines and local specialties amidst the lively atmosphere. (Location: Church Lane, Galway)

5. Cork's Coal Quay Market, Cork: Experience the charm of Cork's Coal Quay Market, where local traders and vendors come together to create a lively marketplace.

From traditional Irish fare to international street food, the market invites you to explore a tapestry of flavors. (Location: Cornmarket Street, Cork City)

6. Street Food at Events and Festivals: Keep an eye out for street food vendors at events and festivals taking place throughout Southern Ireland. Whether it's a music festival, cultural event, or food festival, you're likely to find a diverse range of street food options to tantalize your taste buds.

7. International Influences: Southern Ireland's street food scene embraces international influences, offering a fusion of flavors. From Asian-inspired noodle dishes to Middle Eastern falafel wraps, you can embark on a global culinary journey without leaving the vibrant streets of Ireland.

8. Local Markets Beyond Cities: Venture beyond the city limits to discover local markets in smaller towns and villages. These markets often feature regional produce, homemade treats, and street food offerings, providing a taste of Southern

Ireland's culinary diversity in a more intimate setting.

Southern Ireland's street food and markets are a celebration of flavors, aromas, and the rich tapestry of culinary traditions. Whether you're exploring city streets or meandering through local markets, each bite promises a delicious adventure that reflects the vibrant spirit of the Emerald Isle.

CHAPTER FIVE
MUST-TRY LOCAL DISHES

Traditional Irish Dishes

Embark on a culinary journey through the heart and history of Southern Ireland by indulging in traditional dishes that have stood the test of time. These time-honored recipes, often rooted in local ingredients and agricultural heritage, offer a taste of the authentic flavors that define Irish cuisine.

1. Irish Stew: A quintessential Irish comfort dish, Irish stew is a hearty concoction of lamb or mutton, potatoes, onions, and carrots. Slow-cooked to perfection, this dish reflects the simplicity and warmth of traditional Irish cooking. Savor a bowl of this soul-soothing stew, often enjoyed with a slice of freshly baked soda bread.

2. Colcannon: Celebrating the humble potato, colcannon is a classic Irish side dish made by combining mashed potatoes with finely chopped kale or cabbage, and often infused with creamy butter. This comforting and flavorsome dish is a staple at Irish tables, especially during festive occasions.

3. Boxty: Boxty is a traditional Irish potato pancake, griddled to golden perfection. Made with grated raw potatoes, mashed potatoes, and flour, boxty has a unique texture and flavor. Enjoy it as a side dish or with various toppings, showcasing the versatility of this beloved Irish delight.

4. Coddle: Hailing from Dublin, coddle is a dish that exemplifies resourcefulness. Made with leftover pork sausages, bacon, potatoes, and onions, coddle is slow-cooked to create a savory and satisfying one-pot wonder. It's a comforting meal that brings families together around the dinner table.

5. Soda Bread: No exploration of Irish cuisine is complete without savoring the iconic Irish soda bread. This quick and easy bread is leavened with baking soda, resulting in a dense yet tender loaf. Enjoy it freshly baked, slathered with Irish butter, for a delightful taste of tradition.

6. Boxty Dumplings: Boxty makes another appearance, this time in the form of dumplings. These savory dumplings are often filled with a mixture of seasoned meats and vegetables, providing a hearty and satisfying meal. Boxty dumplings are a culinary treat that pays homage to Ireland's agricultural roots.

7. Dublin Coddle Pizza: A creative twist on the traditional coddle, the Dublin coddle pizza takes the essence of the classic dish and transforms it into a flavorful pizza topping. Enjoy the rich flavors of coddle on a crispy pizza crust, showcasing the adaptability of Irish culinary traditions.

8. Black and White Pudding: Black and white pudding are Irish breakfast staples that may raise an eyebrow or two for the uninitiated. Black pudding is made with blood, oatmeal, and spices, while white pudding is a milder version without blood. Often served as part of a full Irish breakfast, these sausages provide a unique and savory taste experience.

Explore the rich tapestry of Southern Ireland's culinary heritage through these traditional dishes, where each bite is a connection to the past and a celebration of the flavors that define the Emerald Isle.

Regional Specialties

Delve into the diverse culinary landscape of Southern Ireland by exploring the regional specialties that showcase the unique flavors and culinary traditions of specific areas. From coastal delights to inland favorites, each region offers a distinct gastronomic experience that adds to the rich tapestry of Irish cuisine.

1. Dingle Bay Seafood: Along the rugged coast of County Kerry, Dingle Bay is a haven for seafood enthusiasts. Indulge in fresh catches like Dingle Bay crab, lobster, and locally sourced fish. Restaurants such as Out of the Blue (www.outoftheblue.ie) offer a seafood extravaganza, allowing you to savor the bounty of the Atlantic.

2. Waterford Blaa: Head to the southeast city of Waterford to savor the iconic Waterford blaa. This soft, white bread roll has a unique doughy texture and is often enjoyed with a variety of fillings, from bacon to sausages. Local bakeries, like Barron's Bakery (www.barronsbakery.ie), are renowned for their traditional blaas.

3. Connemara Lamb: Nestled in the scenic landscapes of County Galway, Connemara is celebrated for its succulent lamb. Raised on lush green pastures, Connemara lamb is known for its tender and flavorful meat. Enjoy a taste of this regional specialty at local pubs and restaurants, such as O'Dowd's in Roundstone.

4. Burren Smoked Salmon: Explore the limestone terrain of the Burren in County Clare, where the Burren Smokehouse (www.burrensmokehouse.com) produces exquisite smoked salmon. The cold, clear waters of the Atlantic infuse a unique flavor into the salmon, creating a delicacy that is a must-try for seafood enthusiasts.

5. Kilkenny's Hurling Pie: In the medieval city of Kilkenny, savor the unique Hurling Pie, a homage to the ancient Irish sport of hurling. This hearty pie, often filled with succulent meats and root vegetables, is a comforting and delicious dish that pays tribute to Kilkenny's rich cultural heritage.

6. Donegal Oysters: Along the rugged coastline of Donegal, indulge in the briny goodness of Donegal oysters. Known for their plumpness and distinct flavor, these oysters are a delicacy best enjoyed at local seafood establishments like Nancy's Barn (www.nancysbar.ie) in Ballyliffin.

7. Cork's Butter Museum: In the city of Cork, delve into the history of Ireland's dairy industry with a visit to the Cork Butter Museum (www.corkbutter.museum). Discover the significance of butter production in Cork and the region's contribution to the dairy trade.

8. Belfast's Titanic Menu: In Belfast, explore the culinary legacy of the Titanic with a Titanic-themed menu. Restaurants like

Rayanne House (www.rayannehouse.com) offer a dining experience that replicates the last meal served on the ill-fated ship, providing a unique and historical gastronomic journey.

Embark on a culinary adventure across Southern Ireland, where each region unfolds its own unique specialties. From the coastal delights of Dingle to the traditional Waterford blaas, these regional treasures add a distinctive flavor to the rich tapestry of Irish cuisine.

Vegetarian and Vegan Options

Embrace the growing trend of plant-based dining in Southern Ireland as the culinary landscape evolves to cater to vegetarians and vegans. Discover a variety of flavorful and innovative dishes that celebrate the abundance of fresh, local produce and showcase the creativity of chefs committed to providing diverse and satisfying meat-free options.

1. Dublin's Cornucopia: In the heart of Dublin, Cornucopia (www.cornucopia.ie)

stands as a pioneer in vegetarian and vegan dining. This beloved restaurant offers a bountiful array of plant-based dishes, from hearty mains to delectable desserts, providing a welcoming haven for those seeking meat-free options.

2. Vegan Irish Stew: Experience a plant-based twist on the classic Irish stew. Restaurants and cafes across Southern Ireland, such as The Happy Pear (www.thehappypear.ie) in County Wicklow, serve a vegan rendition that captures the comforting essence of the traditional dish using wholesome plant ingredients.

3. Cork's Paradiso: Paradiso (www.paradiso.restaurant) in Cork has gained acclaim for its innovative vegetarian and vegan cuisine. With a focus on bold flavors and inventive combinations, this restaurant elevates plant-based dining to a new level, offering a diverse menu that showcases the best of local produce.

4. Galway's The Light House Café: The Light House Café (www.light-house-cafe.com) in Galway caters to both vegetarians and vegans, providing a welcoming space for plant-based enthusiasts. Explore a menu that features creative salads, hearty mains, and delightful desserts, all crafted with a commitment to sustainability.

5. Plant-Based Pies and Pastries: Many local bakeries and cafes now offer delectable plant-based pies and pastries, providing a tasty option for those seeking a quick and satisfying meal. Check out establishments like The Happy Tart in Belfast or The Happy Pear's bakery for an array of mouthwatering vegan treats.

6. Vegetarian-Friendly Pubs: Pubs across Southern Ireland are increasingly offering vegetarian and vegan options on their menus. Enjoy a cozy evening in establishments like The Barge Pub in Dublin or The Blue Light Pub in County Dublin, where you can find plant-based choices alongside traditional Irish pub fare.

7. Vegan Scones and Treats: Treat your sweet tooth to vegan scones and delightful desserts available at various tearooms and bakeries. Establishments like The Old Barracks Coffee Roastery in Birdhill (www.oldbarracks.ie) or AVOCA Café in multiple locations provide a delightful selection of vegan baked goods.

8. Vegetarian and Vegan Festivals: Explore vegetarian and vegan festivals that occasionally take place across Southern Ireland. These events celebrate plant-based living and offer a variety of food stalls, cooking demonstrations, and informative sessions for those interested in embracing a meat-free lifestyle.

Southern Ireland's culinary scene is becoming increasingly inclusive, with a growing array of vegetarian and vegan options that cater to diverse tastes. Whether you're a committed plant-based enthusiast or simply curious to explore new flavors, the Emerald Isle welcomes you to savor the creativity and deliciousness of its meat-free offerings.

CHAPTER SIX

BUDGET-FRIENDLY ACTIVITIES AND ATTRACTIONS

Free and Low-Cost Attractions

Explore the wonders of Southern Ireland without breaking the bank by discovering a wealth of free and budget-friendly attractions. From natural landscapes to cultural gems, these experiences allow you to immerse yourself in the beauty and history of the region without denting your wallet.

1. Cliffs of Moher Coastal Walk: Marvel at the breathtaking beauty of the Cliffs of Moher with a coastal walk. While there's an entrance fee to access the official Cliffs of Moher Visitor Centre, you can experience the stunning views along the cliff edges for free. Lace up your hiking boots and explore the rugged coastal trail, taking in the Atlantic vistas and dramatic cliffs.

2. National Museums of Ireland: Dive into Ireland's rich history and culture at the

National Museums of Ireland. Explore artifacts, art, and exhibitions covering archaeology, decorative arts, natural history, and more. The National Museum of Ireland – Archaeology in Dublin, with its renowned collection of Celtic and medieval artifacts, offers free admission.

3. St. Stephen's Green, Dublin: Enjoy the tranquility of St. Stephen's Green, a beautiful public park in the heart of Dublin. Stroll through lush greenery, around a picturesque lake, and admire the sculptures and monuments scattered throughout. This peaceful escape provides a serene atmosphere at no cost.

4. Ring of Kerry Scenic Drive: Embark on the Ring of Kerry, one of Ireland's most scenic drives. While there may be some tolls along the route, the majority of the journey offers breathtaking landscapes, charming villages, and coastal views without additional charges. Pack a picnic and take in the natural splendors along this iconic route.

5. Trinity College Dublin Campus: Walk through the historic grounds of Trinity College Dublin, home to the famous Book of Kells. While there's an admission fee to see the Book of Kells exhibition, exploring the beautiful campus, its squares, and the atmospheric Long Room in the Old Library is free.

6. Killarney National Park: Experience the natural beauty of Killarney National Park, where entry is typically free. Explore Muckross House and Gardens, take a stroll around Muckross Lake, or venture into the wooded areas to discover the park's diverse flora and fauna.

7. Galway City Walking Tour: Immerse yourself in the charm of Galway with a self-guided walking tour of the city. Explore Eyre Square, stroll along the Claddagh, and wander through the colorful streets of the Latin Quarter. Many of Galway's attractions, including its vibrant street performances, can be enjoyed without any cost.

8. Dunbrody Famine Ship Experience, New Ross (Low-Cost): While some attractions may have a modest entry fee, they offer excellent value for money. The Dunbrody Famine Ship Experience in New Ross, County Wexford, provides a poignant journey into Ireland's history. Learn about the Great Famine and emigration through interactive exhibits aboard a replica famine ship.

Southern Ireland offers a plethora of free and low-cost attractions, ensuring that you can uncover the beauty, history, and culture of the region without straining your budget. Whether you're exploring the rugged coastlines, historic landmarks, or vibrant cities, these affordable experiences make your journey through the Emerald Isle both enriching and economical.

Outdoor Activities on a Budget

Embrace the natural beauty of Southern Ireland and engage in thrilling outdoor adventures without breaking the bank. Discover a wealth of budget-friendly activities that allow you to experience the region's landscapes, seascapes, and outdoor wonders while keeping your wallet intact.

1. Hiking the Wicklow Mountains: Lace up your hiking boots and explore the scenic trails of the Wicklow Mountains. With a variety of routes suitable for different fitness levels, you can wander through lush valleys, conquer peaks, and witness breathtaking vistas without spending a penny.

2. Kayaking on Lough Leane, Killarney: Dive into the tranquility of Lough Leane in Killarney National Park with budget-friendly kayaking options. Rent a kayak and paddle along the lake, surrounded by picturesque landscapes and the stunning backdrop of the MacGillycuddy's Reeks mountain range.

3. Beach Day in Inchydoney: Enjoy a day of sun, sea, and sand at Inchydoney Beach. This pristine beach in County Cork is perfect for budget-conscious travelers seeking a relaxing day by the Atlantic. Take a leisurely stroll, feel the sand between your toes, or simply bask in the natural beauty of the coastline.

4. Cycling the Great Western Greenway: Discover the beauty of County Mayo by cycling the Great Western Greenway. This 42-kilometer trail, stretching from Westport to Achill Island, offers stunning views of mountains, lakes, and the Atlantic coast. Bring your own bike or rent one locally for an affordable outdoor adventure.

5. Rock Climbing in the Burren: Challenge yourself with rock climbing in the unique limestone landscape of the Burren in County Clare. While guided tours may have a fee, you can explore beginner-friendly routes independently, experiencing the thrill of climbing against the backdrop of this distinctive terrain.

6. Picnic in Glendalough: Immerse yourself in the beauty of Glendalough in County Wicklow with a budget-friendly picnic. Pack a lunch and relax by the picturesque lakes surrounded by lush greenery and ancient monastic ruins. It's a serene way to experience the charm of this historic valley.

7. Fishing at Lough Corrib: Cast your line into the waters of Lough Corrib in County Galway, renowned for its excellent fishing opportunities. Engage in angling from the shoreline or hire an affordable boat to explore the lake's bountiful fishing spots, making for a relaxing and budget-friendly day by the water.

8. Geocaching Adventures: Embark on a treasure hunt with geocaching, a cost-effective and adventurous outdoor activity. Explore Southern Ireland's landscapes while searching for hidden caches using GPS coordinates. It's a unique and budget-friendly way to experience both urban and rural areas.

Southern Ireland's outdoor wonders beckon you to explore, and with these budget-friendly activities, you can immerse yourself in the region's natural splendor without exceeding your travel budget. Whether you're hiking through mountains, paddling on lakes, or enjoying a beach day, the Emerald Isle offers a wealth of outdoor experiences that won't cost you a fortune.

Cultural Experiences without Breaking the Bank

Immerse yourself in the rich tapestry of Southern Ireland's cultural heritage with these affordable and engaging experiences. From historic landmarks to traditional performances, discover the essence of Irish culture without straining your budget.

1. Dublin's Free Museums: Explore Dublin's cultural treasures without spending a penny at the city's many free museums. The National Gallery of Ireland, the National Museum of Ireland – Archaeology, and the Chester Beatty Library offer a wealth of art, artifacts, and manuscripts, providing a budget-friendly dive into Irish history and culture.

2. Traditional Irish Music Sessions: Delight in the soul-stirring tunes of traditional Irish music at local pubs. Many establishments host free music sessions, allowing you to experience the lively and authentic sounds of fiddles, bodhráns, and tin whistles. Check out popular spots like The Cobblestone in Dublin or Tigh Neachtain in Galway for a musical treat.

3. Street Performances in Temple Bar: Wander through Dublin's vibrant Temple Bar district, where street performers bring the streets to life. From talented musicians to entertaining street artists, these impromptu performances provide a lively and cost-free cultural experience.

4. Free Walking Tours: Join free walking tours in cities like Dublin, Cork, and Galway to delve into the local culture and history. Knowledgeable guides lead you through iconic landmarks, sharing fascinating stories and insights. While tipping is appreciated, these tours offer an affordable way to discover the cultural richness of each city.

5. Literary Dublin Tour: Embark on a literary journey through Dublin, exploring the haunts of renowned Irish writers like

James Joyce and Samuel Beckett. Visit spots such as Trinity College's Long Room and the Dublin Writers Museum for a self-guided tour celebrating Ireland's literary heritage.

6. Explore Kilkenny's Medieval Mile: Wander through Kilkenny's Medieval Mile, a historic trail that showcases the city's medieval architecture and heritage. Stroll along cobbled streets, visit landmarks like Kilkenny Castle (entrance fees may apply), and appreciate the charm of this well-preserved medieval city.

7. Galway's Spanish Arch and Claddagh Ring Museum: Visit Galway's Spanish Arch, a historic structure dating back to the 16th century, and explore the nearby Claddagh Ring Museum. While there may be fees for specific exhibitions, the surrounding area provides a picturesque setting to absorb the city's maritime history.

8. Traditional Storytelling Nights: Experience the art of Irish storytelling at cultural events or local pubs that host traditional storytelling nights. Listen to captivating tales passed down through generations, providing insight into Irish folklore, myths, and legends.

Southern Ireland's cultural experiences are not only enriching but also accessible to budget-conscious travelers. Whether you're exploring museums, enjoying traditional music, or soaking in the literary atmosphere, these activities offer a glimpse into the heart and soul of Ireland without breaking the bank.

CHAPTER SEVEN

BUDGET-FRIENDLY TRAVEL ITINERARIES

One-Week Budget Itinerary for Southern Ireland

Discover the enchanting landscapes, rich history, and vibrant culture of Southern Ireland on a budget-friendly one-week itinerary. This carefully crafted plan ensures you make the most of your time without straining your wallet, offering a delightful blend of outdoor adventures, cultural explorations, and culinary delights.

Day 1: Arrival in Dublin

- **Morning:** Explore Dublin's city center on foot. Visit Trinity College for a glimpse of the Book of Kells (admission fee applies) and wander through St. Stephen's Green.

- **Afternoon:** Enjoy a budget-friendly lunch at a local eatery. Head to Temple

Bar for a stroll and take in the lively atmosphere.

- **Evening:** Immerse yourself in the musical scene with a visit to a pub hosting a traditional Irish music session.

Day 2: Wicklow Mountains National Park

- **Morning:** Take an early bus to Glendalough in the Wicklow Mountains. Hike around the Glendalough Valley, exploring the ancient monastic site and the picturesque lakes.

- **Afternoon:** Picnic in the park or enjoy a budget-friendly meal at a local cafe. Continue hiking or relax by the lakeside.

- **Evening:** Return to Dublin and opt for a low-cost dinner in the city center.

Day 3: Galway City

- **Morning:** Travel to Galway by bus or train. Begin your day with a stroll along the Claddagh and the Spanish Arch.
- **Afternoon:** Explore Eyre Square and nearby attractions. Have lunch at a budget-friendly local eatery.
- **Evening:** Attend a free street performance in Galway and savor an affordable dinner at one of the city's many pubs.

Day 4: The Burren and Cliffs of Moher

- **Morning:** Take a bus to the Burren in County Clare. Explore the unique limestone landscape and visit Poulnabrone Dolmen.
- **Afternoon:** Continue to the Cliffs of Moher (entrance fee applies) for stunning coastal views. Pack a picnic to enjoy at the cliffs.
- **Evening:** Return to Galway and dine at a budget-friendly restaurant.

Day 5: Killarney National Park

- **Morning:** Travel to Killarney by bus or train. Spend the morning exploring Muckross House and Gardens.
- **Afternoon:** Rent a bike and cycle through Killarney National Park, taking in the scenic beauty.
- **Evening:** Enjoy a low-cost dinner in Killarney town center.

Day 6: Dingle Peninsula

- **Morning:** Take a bus to Dingle. Explore the charming town and enjoy the local ambiance.
- **Afternoon:** Take a budget-friendly boat tour to see Dingle's coastline and possibly spot dolphins.
- **Evening:** Savor affordable seafood in one of Dingle's eateries.

Day 7: Cork City

- **Morning:** Travel to Cork by bus or train. Visit the English Market and sample some local delights.

- **Afternoon:** Explore Cork's historic sites, such as St. Fin Barre's Cathedral and the Cork City Gaol (admission fees may apply).
- **Evening:** Conclude your journey with a budget-friendly dinner in the city center.

This one-week budget itinerary allows you to experience the diverse landscapes and cultural gems of Southern Ireland without compromising on your wallet. Whether exploring cities, hiking in national parks, or enjoying traditional music, your budget-friendly adventure awaits in the Emerald Isle.

Two-Week Budget Itinerary for Southern Ireland

Embark on an extended journey through the captivating landscapes, historic sites, and vibrant culture of Southern Ireland with this two-week budget-friendly itinerary. Immerse yourself in the beauty of the Emerald Isle while keeping your expenses in check, offering a balanced mix of outdoor exploration, cultural experiences, and delightful culinary discoveries.

Week 1: Dublin, Wicklow, and Galway

Day 1-3: Dublin Exploration

- **Day 1: Arrival and City Stroll**
    - Arrive in Dublin, explore the city center, and visit landmarks like Trinity College and St. Stephen's Green.
    - Enjoy a budget-friendly meal in Temple Bar.

- **Day 2: Museums and Literary Dublin**
    - Explore free-entry museums like the National Gallery and delve into Literary Dublin with visits to bookish spots.
    - Attend a traditional Irish music session in a local pub.

- **Day 3: Day Trip to Howth**

- Take a budget-friendly train to Howth for coastal walks and fresh seafood.
- Return to Dublin for a relaxed evening.

Day 4-6: Wicklow Mountains and Glendalough

- **Day 4: Travel to Wicklow**
    - Journey to the Wicklow Mountains, and explore the town of Wicklow.
    - Hike the scenic trails and enjoy the tranquility of the mountains.
- **Day 5: Glendalough Discovery**
    - Head to Glendalough for a day of exploring the monastic site and lakes.
    - Enjoy a budget-friendly picnic amidst the natural beauty.
- **Day 6: Enniskerry and Return to Dublin**

- Visit Powerscourt Estate in Enniskerry (admission fee may apply).
- Return to Dublin for the evening.

Day 7-10: Galway and Cliffs of Moher

- **Day 7: Travel to Galway**
    - Take a bus or train to Galway and explore the city's vibrant streets.
- **Day 8: Aran Islands Day Trip**
    - Opt for a budget-friendly ferry to the Aran Islands, exploring the unique landscapes.
    - Return to Galway for the evening.
- **Day 9: Cliffs of Moher**
    - Take a day trip to the Cliffs of Moher, enjoying the coastal scenery (entrance fee applies).
    - Return to Galway for the night.
- **Day 10: Connemara Exploration**

- Venture into Connemara, experiencing its scenic landscapes and Connemara National Park.
- Savor a budget-friendly dinner in Galway.

Week 2: Killarney, Dingle, and Cork

Day 11-14: Killarney, Dingle, and Cork Exploration

- **Day 11-12: Killarney National Park and Ring of Kerry**
    - Travel to Killarney and explore Muckross House and Gardens.
    - Cycle or hike in Killarney National Park.
    - Embark on a budget-friendly Ring of Kerry scenic drive.
- **Day 13: Dingle Peninsula**
    - Journey to Dingle and explore the charming town.

- Take a boat tour to witness the stunning coastline.
- Enjoy an affordable seafood dinner.
- **Day 14: Cork City and Departure**
  - Travel to Cork, visiting the English Market and notable landmarks.
  - Conclude your journey with a budget-friendly meal in Cork before departure.

This two-week budget itinerary offers a comprehensive exploration of Southern Ireland's diverse landscapes, historical sites, and cultural gems. From the bustling streets of Dublin to the coastal wonders of the Cliffs of Moher and the picturesque towns of Killarney and Dingle, each day promises a budget-friendly adventure in the enchanting Emerald Isle.

Customizing Your Itinerary

Tailoring your Southern Ireland itinerary allows you to create a personalized journey that aligns with your interests, preferences, and budget. Whether you're drawn to outdoor adventures, cultural explorations, or culinary delights, here are tips on customizing your itinerary to make the most of your experience:

1. Define Your Interests:

- Determine your priorities. Are you passionate about history, nature, culture, or cuisine?

- Identify specific activities or attractions that align with your interests, ensuring a more fulfilling and enjoyable journey.

2. Mix and Match Destinations:

- Southern Ireland offers a diverse range of landscapes and experiences. Mix city exploration with rural getaways to strike a balance.

- Choose destinations that resonate with you, whether it's the vibrant streets of Dublin, the scenic beauty of the Ring of

Kerry, or the cultural ambiance of Galway.

3. Consider Seasonal Variations:

- Be mindful of seasonal changes. Certain activities or attractions may be more appealing during specific times of the year.

- Plan outdoor adventures in milder weather and cultural experiences during festivals or events.

4. Budget-Friendly Accommodations:

- Research affordable accommodation options, such as hostels, guesthouses, or budget-friendly hotels.

- Consider staying in diverse areas, like city centers and smaller towns, for a more varied experience.

5. Optimize Transportation:

- Choose cost-effective transportation options, including buses, trains, or budget airlines for longer journeys.

- Plan routes efficiently to minimize travel time and expenses.

6. Prioritize Free and Low-Cost Activities:

- Identify free and low-cost attractions and activities to manage expenses.
- Look for museums with free entry days, self-guided walking tours, or natural sites that don't require admission fees.

7. Explore Local Cuisine on a Budget:

- Savor local flavors without overspending. Seek out affordable eateries, street food markets, and regional specialties.
- Embrace the culinary scene with a mix of casual and traditional dining experiences.

8. Allow Flexibility in Your Schedule:

- Leave room for spontaneity. Unexpected discoveries and recommendations from locals can enhance your experience.

- Be flexible with your itinerary to adapt to changing weather conditions or unforeseen opportunities.

9. Connect with Locals:

- Engage with locals for insider tips and recommendations. Attend community events or join group activities to immerse yourself in the local culture.

- Participate in guided tours led by locals for a more authentic experience.

10. Capture Memorable Moments:

- Prioritize experiences that resonate with you rather than adhering strictly to a checklist.

- Capture memories through photos, journaling, or other creative outlets to remember the unique aspects of your journey.

Customizing your itinerary ensures that your Southern Ireland adventure aligns with your preferences and allows for a more immersive and fulfilling travel experience. Whether you're seeking cultural insights, natural wonders, or culinary delights, tailor your journey to create lasting memories in the Emerald Isle.

CHAPTER EIGHT

MONEY-SAVING TRAVEL HACKS

Discounts and Deals

Make the most of your budget-friendly journey through Southern Ireland by taking advantage of various discounts and deals. Whether you're exploring cities, enjoying outdoor activities, or savoring local cuisine, these tips will help you maximize your savings and enhance your travel experience.

1. Heritage Cards:

- Invest in a Heritage Card, granting you access to many OPW-managed heritage sites across Ireland. Enjoy free entry or discounted rates at castles, abbeys, and historical landmarks.

2. Free Museum Days:

- Plan your visits to museums on designated free entry days. Many cultural institutions in major cities offer complimentary admission on specific weekdays or times.

3. Student and Youth Discounts:

- If you're a student or a young traveler, carry your student ID or youth card. Many attractions, accommodations, and transportation services offer discounted rates for students and youth.

4. Public Transportation Passes:

- Invest in public transportation passes for cities like Dublin, Cork, and Galway. These passes often provide unlimited travel within a specified timeframe, offering convenience and cost savings.

5. City Tourism Cards:

- Explore city-specific tourism cards that offer discounts on attractions, tours, and dining. These cards, available in major urban centers, can be a valuable investment for budget-conscious travelers.

6. Budget Accommodation Memberships:

- Join budget accommodation networks or loyalty programs to access exclusive discounts. Hostel memberships and online platforms often offer reduced rates for members.

7. Online Booking Platforms:

- Utilize online booking platforms to secure discounted rates on accommodations, activities, and transportation. Platforms like Hostelworld, Booking.com, and Skyscanner often feature special deals and promotions.

8. Group Discounts:

- If you're traveling with a group, inquire about group discounts for tours, attractions, and accommodations. Many providers offer reduced rates for larger groups.

9. Outdoor Activity Bundles:

- Look for bundled packages for outdoor activities. Providers offering activities like kayaking, hiking, or cycling often provide discounts when you book multiple experiences together.

10. Restaurant Specials and Lunch Deals:

- Explore local dining options during lunchtime when many restaurants offer special deals and discounted menus. This is a great way to savor local cuisine without breaking the bank.

11. City Passes:

- Investigate city passes that combine admission to multiple attractions at a reduced price. These passes often include popular sites, guided tours, and public transportation.

12. Festival and Event Promotions:

- If your travel coincides with local festivals or events, check for promotions and discounts. Some events offer reduced rates on accommodations, tickets, or special packages.

13. Senior Citizen Discounts:

- If you're a senior traveler, inquire about senior citizen discounts at attractions, transportation services, and accommodations.

14. Travel During Off-Peak Seasons:

- Plan your trip during off-peak seasons to take advantage of lower prices on accommodations, activities, and tours.

By strategically utilizing discounts and deals, you can stretch your budget further while enjoying all that Southern Ireland has to offer. Whether you're exploring historic sites, indulging in local cuisine, or embarking on outdoor adventures, these savings tips enhance your travel experience in the Emerald Isle.

Budget-Friendly Shopping Tips

Explore the local markets, boutiques, and craft shops of Southern Ireland while staying within your budget. Here are some savvy shopping tips to help you make the most of your shopping experience without overspending:

1. Visit Local Markets:

- Explore local markets like Dublin's Temple Bar Food Market or Cork's English Market. These markets offer a diverse range of fresh produce, handmade crafts, and unique souvenirs at affordable prices.

2. Souvenir Hunting:

- Look for budget-friendly souvenirs, such as locally produced chocolates, handmade crafts, or small trinkets. Avoid tourist traps and opt for items that reflect the region's authentic character.

3. Shop in Off-Peak Hours:

- Visit shops during off-peak hours, especially in popular tourist areas. Shopkeepers may be more willing to negotiate prices, and you'll have a more relaxed shopping experience.

4. Explore Charity Shops:

- Browse charity shops, thrift stores, or second-hand shops for unique finds at a fraction of the price. You might discover vintage clothing, books, or quirky items while supporting a good cause.

5. Take Advantage of Sales:

- Keep an eye out for sales and discounts, especially during seasonal clearances. Many shops offer substantial discounts on clothing, accessories, and homeware.

6. Bargain at Craft Markets:

- When shopping at craft markets or from local artisans, don't hesitate to negotiate prices, especially if you're buying multiple items. Many craftsmen appreciate the direct interaction and may offer discounts.

7. VAT Refund Scheme:

- If you're a non-European Union (EU) resident, explore the Value Added Tax (VAT) refund scheme. Certain shops allow you to reclaim the VAT on eligible purchases, providing additional savings.

8. Shop for Local Products:

- Prioritize locally produced goods and products. These items are often more affordable and make for meaningful souvenirs that support the regional economy.

9. Set a Shopping Budget:

- Establish a shopping budget before you start exploring. This helps you prioritize purchases and prevents overspending on impulse buys.

10. Look for Student Discounts:

- If you're a student, inquire about student discounts at clothing stores, bookshops, and other retail outlets. Many shops offer reduced rates upon presentation of a valid student ID.

11. Explore Outlet Stores:

- Check out outlet stores for discounted prices on clothing, footwear, and accessories. Outlet malls or designated outlet areas in cities often feature well-known brands at lower prices.

12. DIY Picnic Supplies:

- If you plan on having a picnic, consider buying fresh produce and snacks from local markets. This not only supports local vendors but also provides a budget-friendly alternative to dining out.

13. Compare Prices Online:

- Before making a purchase, compare prices online to ensure you're getting a fair deal. Some shops may offer online discounts or promotions that you can take advantage of.

14. Avoid Tourist-Centric Areas:

- Venture beyond tourist-centric areas for shopping. Prices may be more reasonable in neighborhoods where locals shop, providing a more authentic experience.

Smart shopping in Southern Ireland involves exploring local markets, taking advantage of discounts, and embracing the unique products the region has to offer. With these budget-friendly shopping tips, you can curate a collection of souvenirs and treasures without straining your travel budget in the Emerald Isle.

Saving on Souvenirs

Bringing home souvenirs from Southern Ireland doesn't have to strain your budget. Discover budget-friendly ways to commemorate your journey and share the charm of the Emerald Isle with these savvy tips for saving on souvenirs:

1. Local Markets and Craft Fairs:

- Explore local markets and craft fairs where you can find unique, handmade souvenirs at more affordable prices than tourist-oriented shops.

2. Support Local Artisans:

- Purchase directly from local artisans. Items crafted by hand often come with more reasonable price tags, and you'll have the chance to meet the creators.

3. Budget-Friendly Keepsakes:

- Opt for smaller, budget-friendly keepsakes such as keychains, magnets, or postcards. These items are not only cost-effective but also easy to transport.

4. Off-Peak Shopping:

- Shop during off-peak hours to avoid the crowds. This may give you the opportunity to negotiate prices with vendors or discover sales and discounts.

5. Authentic Irish Products:

- Seek out authentic Irish products that represent the local culture and heritage. These items often have more reasonable price points compared to generic tourist souvenirs.

6. Local Foods as Souvenirs:

- Consider purchasing local foods as souvenirs. Irish chocolates, jams, or teas make delightful gifts and are often more budget-friendly than traditional trinkets.

7. Visit Outlet Stores:

- Explore outlet stores for branded items at discounted prices. Outlet malls or designated areas in cities can be treasure troves for finding quality souvenirs without the hefty price tags.

8. Student and Youth Discounts:

- If you're a student or youth traveler, inquire about discounts. Many shops offer reduced rates for students, providing a budget-friendly option for souvenirs.

9. Avoid Tourist Traps:

- Steer clear of tourist traps and souvenir shops in heavily frequented areas. Venture into local neighborhoods where prices may be more reasonable and the selection more diverse.

10. DIY Souvenirs:

- Create your own souvenirs by collecting mementos from your travels, such as pressed flowers, small rocks, or shells. Craft a personalized scrapbook or display to commemorate your journey.

11. Shop at Charity Shops:

- Browse charity shops for hidden gems. These shops often carry second-hand souvenirs and unique items that won't break the bank.

12. Set a Souvenir Budget:

- Establish a souvenir budget before you start shopping. This helps you prioritize purchases and prevents overspending on impulse buys.

13. VAT Refund Scheme:

- Take advantage of the Value Added Tax (VAT) refund scheme if you're a non-European Union resident. This allows you to reclaim the VAT on eligible purchases, providing additional savings.

14. Compare Prices:

- Before making a purchase, compare prices at different shops. Some items may be available at a more affordable rate in less touristy areas.

Souvenir shopping in Southern Ireland can be both enjoyable and budget-friendly with a bit of strategic planning. Whether you're opting for handmade crafts, local delicacies, or budget-friendly trinkets, these tips will help you bring home cherished mementos without overspending.

CHAPTER NINE
SAFETY TIPS FOR BUDGET TRAVELERS

Staying Safe in Southern Ireland

Southern Ireland is known for its warm hospitality and friendly atmosphere, making it a generally safe destination for travelers. However, like any place, it's essential to stay vigilant and informed to ensure a safe and enjoyable experience. Here are key tips for staying safe in Southern Ireland:

1. Emergency Services:

- Familiarize yourself with emergency contact numbers. In Southern Ireland, the emergency services number is 112 or 999.

2. Health Precautions:

- Ensure you have travel insurance that covers medical expenses. Carry any necessary medications, and be aware of the location of hospitals and pharmacies.

3. Weather Awareness:

- Stay informed about the weather conditions, especially if you plan on engaging in outdoor activities. Ireland's weather can be unpredictable, so bring appropriate clothing and be prepared for rain.

4. Public Transportation Safety:

- If using public transportation, be cautious with personal belongings and keep an eye on your surroundings. Use reputable transportation services and licensed taxis.

5. Road Safety:

- If driving, familiarize yourself with local traffic rules. Ireland drives on the left side of the road. Exercise caution on rural roads, and be mindful of pedestrians and cyclists.

6. Drink Responsibly:

- If enjoying the local pubs and nightlife, drink responsibly. Be cautious of your alcohol intake and never leave drinks unattended.

7. Water Safety:

- If partaking in water activities, adhere to safety guidelines. Be aware of currents, tides, and weather conditions. Always use proper equipment, such as life jackets.

8. Avoid Risky Areas:

- Exercise caution in unfamiliar or poorly lit areas, especially at night. Avoid displaying valuable items openly, and keep an eye on your belongings in crowded places.

9. Stay Informed:

- Stay informed about local news and any travel advisories. Follow the guidance of local authorities and be aware of your surroundings.

10. Emergency Contacts:

- Keep a list of emergency contacts, including your country's embassy or consulate. Inform someone trustworthy about your travel plans.

11. Respect Local Customs:

- Familiarize yourself with local customs and cultural norms. Respect the traditions and practices of the local community to avoid unintentional misunderstandings.

12. Wildlife Precautions:

- If exploring natural areas, be aware of local wildlife. Keep a safe distance and follow any guidelines provided by authorities or park officials.

13. Cybersecurity:

- Exercise caution with online activities. Use secure Wi-Fi connections, avoid sharing sensitive information, and be mindful of cybersecurity risks.

14. Trust Your Instincts:

- Trust your instincts. If a situation feels uncomfortable or unsafe, remove yourself from it. Always prioritize your well-being.

Southern Ireland's welcoming communities and stunning landscapes await your exploration. By staying informed, being aware of your surroundings, and taking necessary precautions, you can ensure a safe and enjoyable journey through the Emerald Isle.

Emergency Contacts and Resources

While Southern Ireland is generally a safe destination, it's essential to be prepared and familiarize yourself with emergency contacts and resources. In case of any unforeseen situations, having access to the right information can be crucial. Here's a guide to emergency contacts and resources in Southern Ireland:

1. Emergency Services:
- For immediate assistance in emergencies, dial 112 or 999. These numbers connect you to police, fire,

ambulance, and other emergency services.

2. Medical Assistance:

- If you require medical assistance, contact the local hospital or medical center. In case of a serious emergency, call for an ambulance by dialing 112 or 999.

3. Police Services:

- To report non-emergency incidents or seek assistance from the police, contact the local Gardaí station. The general contact number for the Gardaí is 1800 666 111.

4. Consular Assistance:

- If you are a foreign traveler and require consular assistance, contact your country's embassy or consulate. Keep their contact information handy, including the local address and phone number.

5. Traveler's Assistance:

- Reach out to local tourist information centers or travel assistance services for guidance on accommodations, transportation, or any travel-related concerns.

6. Roadside Assistance:

- If you encounter issues with your vehicle, contact the appropriate roadside assistance service. Note the contact details provided by your rental car company or use local services.

7. Health and Medical Information:

- For health-related information, consult local medical professionals or hospitals. The Health Service Executive (HSE) in Ireland provides valuable health resources and information.

8. Local Authorities:

- In case of non-emergency situations or to report local issues, contact the local authorities. This may include municipal offices, environmental agencies, or other relevant departments.

9. Lost or Stolen Items:

- If you lose personal belongings or experience theft, report the incident to the local police station. Obtain a copy of the report for insurance or replacement purposes.

10. Wildlife or Environmental Emergencies:

- For emergencies related to wildlife or the environment, contact relevant local authorities or conservation organizations. They can provide guidance on how to handle situations involving wildlife.

11. Mental Health Support:

- If you require mental health support, contact local mental health services or hotlines. In Ireland, organizations like Samaritans provide confidential support.

12. Tourist Information Centers:

- Visit local tourist information centers for assistance, maps, and information about the region. These centers can be valuable resources for travelers.

13. Online Resources:

- Utilize online resources such as government websites, travel forums, and official tourism websites for the latest information on safety, travel advisories, and local services.

14. Travel Insurance Provider:

- Keep the contact information for your travel insurance provider readily available. In case of emergencies or medical issues, your insurance provider can offer guidance on coverage and assistance.

Before your journey, make a list of these emergency contacts and resources. Keep a copy in your travel documents and share it with a trusted friend or family member. Being prepared ensures that you can navigate any unforeseen circumstances with confidence during your travels in Southern Ireland.

CHAPTER TEN

USEFUL RESOURCES

Budget Travel Websites

Navigating the budget-friendly landscape of Southern Ireland becomes even more accessible with the help of specialized websites designed to cater to the needs of savvy travelers. Explore these budget travel websites to streamline your journey and discover valuable insights:

1. Hostelworld (hostelworld.com):

- Ideal for budget-conscious travelers, Hostelworld offers an extensive database of hostels, guesthouses, and budget accommodations. Browse reviews, compare prices, and book affordable stays in various locations across Southern Ireland.

2. Skyscanner (skyscanner.net):

- Skyscanner is your go-to platform for finding budget-friendly flights, hotels, and car rentals. Utilize its search features to discover the most economical travel options to and within Southern Ireland.

3. Rome2Rio (rome2rio.com):

- Rome2Rio provides comprehensive transportation options, including buses, trains, and flights. Plan your route, compare costs, and optimize your travel expenses when moving between destinations in Southern Ireland.

4. GoEuro (omio.com):

- Now known as Omio, this platform specializes in comparing and booking various transportation modes, including trains, buses, and flights. Optimize your travel routes and save money on transportation within Southern Ireland.

5. Booking.com (booking.com):

- Booking.com is a versatile platform offering budget-friendly accommodations, including hotels, hostels, and guesthouses. Explore user reviews, filter by price range, and secure cost-effective stays across different regions.

6. BlaBlaCar (blablacar.com):

- For a unique and cost-effective travel experience, consider BlaBlaCar. This rideshare platform connects drivers with available seats to passengers traveling in the same direction, offering an affordable alternative to traditional transportation.

7. Budget Your Trip (budgetyourtrip.com):

- Budget Your Trip provides estimated daily travel costs based on user data, helping you plan and manage your budget effectively. Get insights into the expected expenses for accommodation, meals, transportation, and activities in Southern Ireland.

8. HappyCow (happycow.net):

- Ideal for budget-conscious foodies, HappyCow is a valuable resource for finding vegetarian, vegan, and budget-friendly dining options in Southern Ireland. Explore reviews and discover local eateries that align with your preferences.

9. Hopper (hopper.com):

- Hopper specializes in predicting and monitoring flight prices, allowing you to book tickets when fares are at their lowest. Use Hopper to find budget-friendly flights to and from Southern Ireland.

10. Workaway (workaway.info):

- For travelers open to exchanging work for accommodation, Workaway is an excellent platform. Browse opportunities in Southern Ireland, connect with hosts, and experience the region in a unique and cost-effective way.

11. Couchsurfing (couchsurfing.com):

- Couchsurfing connects travelers with locals willing to offer free accommodation. Immerse yourself in the local culture, make new friends, and enjoy a budget-friendly stay in Southern Ireland.

12. TripAdvisor (tripadvisor.com):

- TripAdvisor offers a wealth of information on accommodations, restaurants, and attractions. Read reviews, get insights from fellow travelers, and make informed decisions to stretch your budget while exploring Southern Ireland.

13. Wikitravel (wikitravel.org):

- Wikitravel provides user-generated travel guides with valuable tips on budget-friendly accommodations, dining options, and activities in various regions, including Southern Ireland.

14. Nomadic Matt (nomadicmatt.com):

- Nomadic Matt's website offers practical advice, budget travel tips, and destination guides. Explore the Southern Ireland section for insights into cost-effective travel experiences.

These budget travel websites serve as valuable tools for planning, optimizing expenses, and making the most of your journey through Southern Ireland. Whether you're seeking affordable accommodations, transportation deals, or budget-friendly dining options, these platforms empower you to navigate the Emerald Isle without compromising on experiences.

Recommended Reading

Enrich your journey through Southern Ireland by delving into literature that captures the essence, history, and culture of this enchanting region. Here's a curated list of recommended reading to enhance your understanding and appreciation of the Emerald Isle:

1. "Dubliners" by James Joyce:

- This collection of short stories by James Joyce provides a vivid portrayal of Dublin life in the early 20th century. Joyce's masterful prose offers a literary journey through the streets and neighborhoods of the Irish capital.

2. "Angela's Ashes" by Frank McCourt:

- Frank McCourt's memoir recounts his childhood in Limerick, offering a poignant and humorous reflection on poverty, family, and resilience. The narrative provides a personal insight into Irish life in the mid-20th century.

3. "Trinity" by Leon Uris:

- "Trinity" is a historical novel that spans generations, exploring Ireland's struggle for independence and the complexities of identity. Leon Uris weaves a captivating tale against the backdrop of key events in Irish history.

4. "The Picture of Dorian Gray" by Oscar Wilde:

- Oscar Wilde's classic novel takes readers into the decadent world of Victorian Dublin. The story of Dorian Gray's moral descent unfolds against the backdrop of Wilde's sharp wit and social commentary.

5. "Ireland" by Frank Delaney:

- In "Ireland," Frank Delaney skillfully weaves together myths, legends, and historical events to create a rich tapestry of Irish storytelling. The novel explores the impact of storytelling on individual lives and the nation's collective memory.

6. "The Quiet Man" by Maurice Walsh:

- Maurice Walsh's short story "The Quiet Man" provides a glimpse into rural Irish life. The tale, set in the picturesque landscape of County Mayo, has been adapted into a beloved film capturing the charm of Irish traditions.

7. "The Commitments" by Roddy Doyle:

- Roddy Doyle's novel introduces readers to the vibrant music scene of Dublin. "The Commitments" follows a group of young musicians as they strive to create the ultimate soul band in the heart of the city.

8. "How the Irish Saved Civilization" by Thomas Cahill:

- Thomas Cahill explores the role of Irish monks in preserving classical knowledge during the Dark Ages. "How the Irish Saved Civilization" sheds light on Ireland's historical contributions to education and culture.

9. "Normal People" by Sally Rooney:

- Sally Rooney's modern novel delves into the complexities of relationships and identity among Irish youth. Set against the backdrop of Dublin and County Sligo, "Normal People" offers a contemporary exploration of love and friendship.

10. "The Sea" by John Banville: - John Banville's novel, which won the Man Booker

Prize, unfolds along the Irish coast. "The Sea" reflects on memory, loss, and the passage of time through the introspective narrative of its protagonist.

Whether you're seeking historical depth, contemporary insights, or the magic of Irish storytelling, these recommended readings offer a diverse and enriching literary journey through Southern Ireland. Each book provides a unique lens through which to view the landscapes, history, and people that shape the captivating allure of the Emerald Isle.

CHAPTER ELEVEN
CONCLUSION

Encouragement for Budget Travelers

Embarking on a budget-friendly journey through Southern Ireland is not just a financial choice; it's a pathway to immersive experiences, unexpected discoveries, and a deeper connection with the local culture. As you navigate the Emerald Isle on a budget, here's some encouragement to enhance your travel adventure:

1. Embrace the Thrill of Discovery:

- Every budget traveler is a modern-day explorer, venturing off the beaten path to discover hidden gems and authentic local experiences. Embrace the thrill of the unknown and savor the joy of stumbling upon unexpected treasures.

2. Connect with Locals:

- Budget travel often leads to more meaningful interactions with locals.

Engage in conversations, ask for recommendations, and immerse yourself in the warm hospitality of Southern Ireland. The stories shared by locals can be as enriching as the historic sites you visit.

3. Prioritize Experiences Over Things:

- While souvenir shopping is enticing, the memories you create and the experiences you have will last a lifetime. Prioritize activities, cultural encounters, and adventures that leave a lasting impact on your travel narrative.

4. Enjoy the Culinary Adventure:

- Southern Ireland's culinary scene is not just about Michelin-starred restaurants; it's about savoring the rich flavors of local markets, street food, and traditional dishes. Delight in the gastronomic adventure that fits your budget.

5. Seek Budget-Friendly Accommodations:

- Budget accommodations, whether hostels, guesthouses, or B&Bs, offer a chance to connect with fellow travelers. The communal atmosphere fosters friendships, shared experiences, and the camaraderie of like-minded individuals.

6. Capture the Essence of Nature:

- Ireland's landscapes are a masterpiece, and many of the most breathtaking views are accessible without breaking the bank. Explore national parks, hike coastal trails, and relish the beauty of the natural world around you.

7. Embrace the Unpredictability:

- Budget travel invites a certain level of spontaneity. Embrace the unpredictability, allowing room for unexpected adventures, last-minute decisions, and the freedom to go where the journey takes you.

8. Cherish Budget-Friendly Moments:

- Whether it's a simple picnic in a park, a sunset stroll, or a budget-friendly local performance, cherish the moments that don't require a hefty price tag. Often, it's these simple pleasures that become the highlights of your journey.

9. Build Resilience and Resourcefulness:

- Budget travel teaches resilience and resourcefulness. From navigating public transportation to finding creative ways to stretch your budget, each challenge becomes an opportunity for personal growth and adaptability.

10. Create Your Own Narrative:

- Your budget travel story is uniquely yours. It's not about following an itinerary meticulously; it's about crafting your narrative, making choices that resonate with your interests, and creating a travel experience that reflects your individuality.

11. Celebrate the Freedom of Budget Travel:

- Budget travel liberates you from the constraints of luxury and excess. Celebrate the freedom to explore, learn, and indulge in the essence of Southern Ireland without the trappings of opulence.

As a budget traveler in Southern Ireland, you're not just witnessing the beauty of the Emerald Isle; you're actively participating in its vibrant tapestry. Each budget-friendly choice becomes a brushstroke, contributing to a travel masterpiece that is uniquely yours. Embrace the journey, relish the moments, and let the spirit of adventure guide you through the enchanting landscapes of Southern Ireland.

Resources for Further Exploration

Your journey through Southern Ireland is just the beginning of a rich tapestry waiting to be woven. To delve deeper into the culture, history, and wonders of the Emerald Isle, consider these resources for further exploration:

1. Local Libraries and Bookstores:

- Dive into Irish literature and history at local libraries or bookstores. Discover works by renowned authors such as James Joyce, W.B. Yeats, or contemporary writers capturing the essence of Ireland.

2. Historical Museums and Exhibitions:

- Explore historical museums and exhibitions that provide in-depth insights into Ireland's past. The National Museum of Ireland and local heritage centers offer a comprehensive look at the country's rich history.

3. Cultural Events and Festivals:

- Check out local cultural events and festivals that celebrate Irish music, dance, and traditions. Events like the Dublin Literary Festival or traditional music festivals offer a deeper understanding of Ireland's cultural heritage.

4. Online Travel Communities:

- Connect with fellow travelers on online platforms and travel forums. Share experiences, seek advice, and gain valuable insights from those who have explored Southern Ireland. Websites like Lonely Planet's Thorn Tree or Reddit's travel communities are great places to start.

5. Podcasts and Documentaries:

- Immerse yourself in Irish stories and history through podcasts and documentaries. Engaging mediums like "The Irish History Podcast" or documentaries on platforms like National Geographic provide captivating narratives.

6. Local Art Galleries:

- Explore local art galleries to appreciate contemporary Irish art. From traditional paintings to modern installations, these spaces offer a glimpse into Ireland's evolving artistic scene.

7. Language Learning Apps:

- Enhance your travel experience by learning a bit of the Irish language (Gaeilge). Language learning apps like Duolingo or Babbel can introduce you to basic phrases, adding a linguistic layer to your exploration.

8. Nature and Wildlife Guides:

- Delve deeper into Ireland's diverse landscapes and wildlife with nature guides. Books or online resources focused on Ireland's flora and fauna enhance your appreciation for the natural beauty surrounding you.

9. Local Traditional Music Sessions:

- Attend local traditional music sessions in pubs or cultural venues. Immerse yourself in the melodic traditions of Irish folk music and discover the unique instruments and tunes that define the country's musical heritage.

10. Online Courses on Irish History and Culture:

- Enroll in online courses that delve into Irish history, culture, and folklore. Platforms like Coursera or edX often offer courses created by renowned institutions that allow you to deepen your understanding from the comfort of your home.

11. Regional Tourist Information Centers:

- Visit regional tourist information centers for brochures, maps, and additional resources. Knowledgeable staff can provide recommendations for specific areas, ensuring you make the most of your journey.

12. Eco-Tourism Initiatives:

- Explore eco-tourism initiatives that highlight sustainable practices and conservation efforts in Southern

Ireland. Learn about local initiatives that promote responsible travel and environmental awareness.

13. Explore Nearby Islands:

- Consider venturing to nearby islands, such as the Aran Islands or the Skellig Islands. Each island offers a unique perspective on Irish history, heritage, and natural beauty.

14. Historical Walking Tours:

- Join historical walking tours in cities and towns. Knowledgeable guides share fascinating anecdotes, providing a more immersive experience as you stroll through centuries-old streets.

These resources offer a roadmap for further exploration, helping you uncover the layers of Southern Ireland's captivating story. Whether you're delving into literature, attending local events, or connecting with fellow travelers, each resource adds depth to your understanding and appreciation of the Emerald Isle.

Made in the USA
Las Vegas, NV
10 April 2024